Original title:
Feelings in Flight

Copyright © 2024 Creative Arts Management OÜ
All rights reserved.

Author: Nathaniel Blackwood
ISBN HARDBACK: 978-9916-88-958-9
ISBN PAPERBACK: 978-9916-88-959-6

Horizons Painted with Longing

Across the skyline, colors blend,
Dreams stretch far, where hopes ascend.
Waves of feeling brush the shore,
Yearning hearts seek evermore.

Whispers dance in twilight's glow,
Breezes carry tales of woe.
Yet in the dusk, a spark ignites,
Guiding souls through starry nights.

Gentle Currents of Emotion

Softly flowing, hearts collide,
In the river where tears reside.
Secrets linger, softly spoken,
Bond unbreakable, never broken.

Tender moments drift like leaves,
Swaying gently through autumn eves.
With every twist, love's path is clear,
Guided by the currents near.

The Flight of Joyful Shadows

Dancing light beneath the sun,
Shadows play, they laugh and run.
Whirling colors, spirits free,
Chasing dreams, a jubilee.

In the twilight, silhouettes grow,
Joyful secrets ebb and flow.
With each heartbeat, joy expands,
Painting moments, hand in hands.

Nesting in Celestial Dreams

In the quiet of the night,
Dreams take flight, out of sight.
Stars align, a cosmic dance,
Whispers wrapped in sweet romance.

Floating softly, hearts embrace,
Drifting through this endless space.
In stillness, we find our place,
Nesting here, in time's warm grace.

Aetherial Embrace

In twilight's glow, we softly drift,
Through whispers where the starlight lifts.
A dance of shadows, light entwined,
Within the heart, true peace we find.

The moon a guide, so wise and bold,
She wraps our souls in silver gold.
With every breath, we rise and sway,
In harmony, we greet the day.

High Above the Turmoil

Amidst the chaos, we ascend,
Where hopes and dreams begin to blend.
The clouds below a distant sigh,
Up here, our spirits learn to fly.

A realm untouched by earthly pain,
Where laughter dances like the rain.
In heights of calm, our worries cease,
We find our strength, our inner peace.

Liberation Above the Clouds

With wings of light, we break the chains,
In azure skies, love knows no pains.
Each gust a promise, fresh and clear,
A realm where dreams are free from fear.

The thunder's roar fades to a hum,
In quietude, our hearts become.
We rise as one, among the high,
With hopes and dreams that touch the sky.

Mysteries of the Loft

In twilight's glow, secrets unfold,
Whispers of ages, soft and bold.
The stars above, a tapestry,
We seek the truth in silent glee.

Each echo carries tales untold,
Of love and life, both young and old.
In every shadow, light resides,
The mysteries where hope abides.

Wings of Reflection

In silence, reflections soar,
Beneath the vast, unyielding sky.
Whispers of the heart implore,
Dreams take flight, they long to fly.

Shadows dance in evening's glow,
Mirrors of a soul laid bare.
Wings unfurl, they gently flow,
Carried on the breath of air.

Moments slip like grains of sand,
Each a heartbeat, soft and sweet.
With every thought, we understand,
Life's embrace, a fleeting beat.

In the stillness, wisdom waits,
Guiding paths through night and day.
With wings of light, we contemplate,
The journey leads us on our way.

Misty Embrace

Veils of fog wrap the dawn,
Whispers soft as morning mist.
Nature's breath, a gentle yawn,
In the stillness, dreams persist.

Shrouded hills in silence speak,
Crickets lull the world to rest.
In the haze, the shadows sneak,
Nature's hands hold us, caressed.

Every leaf a tale unfolds,
As the sun begins to rise.
In the warmth, the earth beholds,
Life anew, beneath the skies.

Misty tendrils weave around,
Binding hearts in tranquil grace.
In this realm, pure peace is found,
Lost in nature's sweet embrace.

Ephemeral Aspirations

Goals like stars in night's expanse,
Fleeting visions in our mind.
Every thought a daring chance,
An echo of what we might find.

Chasing dreams through fields of hope,
Running fast yet standing still.
Hand in hand, we learn to cope,
With the fire of our own will.

Time, a fabric woven fine,
Threads of gold, moments to seize.
Every heartbeat, life's design,
In the tapestry of dreams.

Fleeting sparks that light the dark,
Illuminating paths unknown.
In our quest, we leave a mark,
Ever onward, seeds are sown.

The Lift of Lament

In shadows deep, the heart does ache,
But from the pain, we learn to rise.
With every tear, the spirits wake,
Finding strength within the cries.

Melodies of sorrow play,
Strings of fate that gently bind.
Through the night, we weave our way,
In the music of the mind.

Lament becomes a guiding light,
Transforming grief to hope anew.
Through the struggle, we take flight,
Emerging strong with skies in view.

Every loss a chance to heal,
In the depths, we find our grace.
From lament, our hearts reveal,
A journey towards a brighter place.

Aerial Reveries

Above the world, the whispers call,
In gentle breezes, we rise and fall.
Clouds like dreams drift far away,
In their soft arms, we long to stay.

Colors blend in twilight's glow,
A canvas vast, a world to sow.
With every breath, we touch the sky,
In aerial realms, our spirits fly.

The Dance of Ascending Hues

In the dawn, a palette wakes,
Soft pinks and golds, the earth it shakes.
With every brush of light's embrace,
A dance of colors, nature's grace.

Spirals twirling, a vivid display,
Painting skies in a bold ballet.
Whispers of joy in every hue,
Ascend with warmth, as dreams renew.

Surrender to the Clouded Embrace

In fog's soft lull, we softly drift,
Wrapped in whispers, a gentle gift.
Clouded dreams that gently sway,
In their embrace, we lose our way.

Voices echo in the mist,
Promises formed, a tender tryst.
Surrender now to what we find,
In the embrace, our hearts unwind.

Driftwood of Hope

On the shore, we gather dreams,
Driftwood stories, tangled themes.
Each piece worn by time and tide,
Carries whispers of hope inside.

In every grain, a tale is spun,
A journey shared by many, one.
With hearts together, we'll create,
A testament of love, not fate.

A Tapestry of Aerial Echoes

In the sky where whispers play,
Colorful threads weave night and day.
Voices dance on gentle breeze,
Echoing tales among the trees.

Stars twinkle in a velvet sea,
Each one holds a memory.
Clouds drift by in silent grace,
Carrying dreams from place to place.

A symphony of flight and sound,
In the heights, life can be found.
Nature's canvas, vast and wide,
A tapestry where hearts abide.

Wings of the Unseen

Invisible wings brush past the ear,
Carrying whispers only few can hear.
In shadows deep, they glide and roam,
Searching for a place called home.

The wind sings softly, secrets held tight,
Guiding lost souls through the night.
A fluttering touch from realms unknown,
In every heart, their presence grown.

They lift us high, yet hold us near,
In moments of joy and tinges of fear.
Though unseen, their strength is clear,
Wings of the unseen, always near.

Wings of Discontent

In skies of gray, the shadows loom,
A weight of sorrow, a gathering gloom.
Wings beat heavy, hearts confined,
Yearning for freedom, yet maligned.

Voices murmur, dreams fall apart,
Each longing strikes like a broken dart.
Chasing horizons, fighting the ground,
In this struggle, hope is found.

But within the ache, a spark persists,
A flicker of light through the swirling mist.
With courage bold, they seek ascent,
Transforming pain into wings of intent.

Soaring Dreams

On the wings of dreams, we take to flight,
Chasing the dawn, embracing the night.
Up in the clouds, where wishes rise,
We pen our hopes in open skies.

With every heartbeat, each breath we share,
Soaring beyond, shedding despair.
Together we venture where few have gone,
In the embrace of a golden dawn.

Winds of change guide us ever forth,
Mapping our journey, for what it's worth.
In the realm of dreams, we are alive,
Soaring high, together we thrive.

Boundless Emotions

In the depths of silence, dreams arise,
Waves of laughter kiss the skies.
Whispers dance on gentle winds,
Hope and joy where love begins.

Moments flicker like the stars,
Binding hearts with invisible bars.
In every tear, a story cries,
Boundless feelings, no goodbyes.

Time flows softly, never spent,
Each heartbeat a sweet lament.
In the fabric of the night,
Emotions blaze, a fiery light.

Together we sail on this sea,
Embracing all that is meant to be.
With every breath, a promise grows,
Boundless love that forever flows.

Gliding through Shadows

Underneath the silver moon,
Whispers glide, a haunting tune.
Reach for love in the darkest night,
Guided by the softest light.

In shadows deep, where echoes play,
Hearts entwined will find their way.
Lost in dreams that softly weave,
Making magic, we believe.

Time stands still in twilight's grace,
Gliding through this secret space.
Here, the silence speaks so loud,
Wrapped in mystery, we're allowed.

Beneath the stars, our spirits soar,
Finding peace, forevermore.
In these shadows, we create,
A love that only dreams can sate.

The Breeze of Longing

A gentle whisper stirs the trees,
Carrying hopes on a soft breeze.
In every sigh, a wish takes flight,
Through the corridors of night.

Longing dances in the air,
Yearning hearts, a secret pair.
Feel the pull of distant dreams,
Life flows gently, or so it seems.

In shadows cast by silver light,
Every heartbeat feels so right.
The breeze carries tales untold,
Of love and warmth against the cold.

Here we stand, in twilight's glow,
Where every breath can love bestow.
Through the passage of the night,
The breeze of longing, pure delight.

Cascading Hearts

Tumbling down like autumn leaves,
Hearts cascade, each one believes.
Cascading dreams in colors bright,
Flowing softly, pure and light.

In the rush of life's embrace,
Fleeting moments find their place.
Every heartbeat, a gentle sigh,
Cascading love will never die.

Through the valleys, over hills,
In the dance of joy, the spirit fills.
With every whisper, the world sways,
As cascading hearts find their ways.

Boundless journeys hand in hand,
In the beauty of love, we stand.
Through the laughter, through the tears,
Cascading hearts throughout the years.

Unraveled by Air

Whispers of breezes softly play,
Dancing leaves in a gentle sway.
Stories told through the rustling sound,
Nature's secrets in silence found.

Threads of dreams in the twilight glow,
Unraveling truths we long to know.
In the vastness where thoughts take flight,
Hope takes form in the fading light.

Cradled by Clouds

Cotton castles float on high,
Soft pillows in a azure sky.
Each step taken on the breeze,
Carried gently with such ease.

Hopes and wishes drift along,
In this realm, we all belong.
Cradled dreams upon the air,
Finding solace everywhere.

Kites of Contentment

Brightly colored, they soar and glide,
In the breezy warmth of the tide.
Tales of laughter, joy, and cheer,
In every pull, the heart draws near.

Strings attached to love's embrace,
As they dance in open space.
Kites of freedom, spirits rise,
Painting colors in the skies.

Wingspan of the Mind

Thoughts unfurl like birds in flight,
With a wingspan that touches light.
Ideas flutter from dusk to dawn,
In the silence, they are drawn.

Imagination takes the lead,
Nurturing every hidden seed.
In this vast expanse we tread,
Wings of wisdom overhead.

Celestial Yearning

Beneath the vast expanse of stars,
I whisper wishes to the night.
With every glint of distant light,
I seek the dreams that feel so far.

The moon's embrace, a tender glow,
Guides my heart through shadowed wane.
I lift my gaze, the cosmos' reign,
Filling my soul with endless flow.

Constellations weave a tale of old,
Of lovers lost and found in space.
In stardust trails, I find my place,
Their secrets in the heavens told.

Each moment drifts like a comet's tail,
A fleeting spark against the night.
With every breath, I chase the light,
In this vast world, I shall not fail.

Resilience in the Air

Through storms that shake the solid ground,
    The heart within must learn to rise.
    With every tear that fills the skies,
A whisper of strength can be found.

The winds may howl, the fears may call,
    But deep inside, a fire glows.
    In darkness, even courage grows,
A spirit strong that will not fall.

Each challenge faced, a lesson learned,
The skies will clear, the sun will shine.
    In every struggle, hope aligns,
As resilience in our hearts burned.

So let the tempest roar and rage,
For I will stand with open arms.
With every storm, I'll find the charms,
    And turn each trial to a page.

A Dance with Dusk

As day retreats in hues of gold,
The shadows stretch and softly play.
In twilight's glow, the world gives way,
To dreams that softly will unfold.

The whispering winds begin to hum,
While stars peek out to kiss the sky.
In this embrace where whispers lie,
My heart leaps forth, the night has come.

A dance between the light and dark,
The moonlight waltzes on the ground.
In gentle steps, lost, I am found,
Awake beneath the evening spark.

Each moment sways like shadows thin,
Composing sights that thrill the soul.
With every breath, I feel more whole,
In this sweet dance where dreams begin.

Beneath the Open Canopy

Beneath the trees, a secret space,
Where sunlight dances on the ground.
In nature's arms, I'm safe, I'm sound,
Embraced by green, a warm embrace.

The leaves above a silent choir,
Each rustle sings of tales untold.
In shades of emerald and gold,
I find the peace that I aspire.

With every breeze, the branches sway,
A melody that soothes the mind.
In this rare haven, joy I find,
Where time slips by, a fleeting day.

So here I linger, heart at ease,
In nature's lap, I feel alive.
With every breath, my spirits thrive,
Beneath this canopy, my peace.

A Journey Beyond the Clouds

Up above the world we climb,
Softly drifting, lost in time.
Whispers of the winds collide,
Carrying dreams on wings of pride.

Golden rays break through the gray,
Painting skies in bright array.
Dancing with the stars so bright,
Guided by the moon's soft light.

Clouds like castles in the air,
Floating freely, void of care.
Echoes of our laughter rise,
As we chase the boundless skies.

With every breath, we feel alive,
In this realm, our spirits thrive.
A journey vast, forever wide,
Beyond the clouds, our hearts reside.

Explorations of Elation

In the meadow, joy's embrace,
Nature's wonders, a boundless space.
Every flower sings a tune,
Beneath the warm and watchful moon.

Rivers dance and trees respond,
In this world, we are so fond.
Chasing echoes, laughter clear,
In the moments we hold dear.

Mountains rise, majestic heights,
Calling forth our daring flights.
Onward, forward, hearts that soar,
Unfolding pathways, evermore.

With every step, new trails we find,
In the explorations of our mind.
Elation pulses through our veins,
In these adventures, love remains.

The Flight of Solitude

In silence, shadows play,
A distant echo calls.
The heart learns to sway,
As twilight softly falls.

Beneath the starry veil,
A whisper through the night.
The dreams begin to sail,
In search of fleeting light.

Each moment feels so vast,
Yet tethered to the ground.
In solitude, the past,
And future both surround.

Through hours that unfold,
A journey finds its way.
In solitude, I'm bold,
In silence, I will stay.

Aerial Reverie

Up high where eagles soar,
The sky unfolds its grace.
With dreams I can't ignore,
  I dance in open space.

The clouds, like painted dreams,
    Encircle my free mind.
   In sunlit golden beams,
I leave the past behind.

With every breath I take,
The freedom fills my soul.
In flight, I gently wake,
And feel completely whole.

Each heartbeat's melody,
A song of pure delight.
In this sweet reverie,
I lift beyond the night.

Flightpaths of Desire

In shadows of the night,
Desires take to the skies.
With passions burning bright,
They weave through whispered sighs.

Each wish a paper plane,
That glides on dreams alone.
In twilight's soft refrain,
I seek the love I've known.

Across the boundless blue,
My heart's compass will steer.
In echoes, I pursue,
The longing drawing near.

With wings of hope I chase,
The starlit paths of fate.
In fervent, warm embrace,
I find what love can create.

Touching the Void

In silence, darkness reigns,
A canvas wide and bare.
With thoughts that twist like chains,
I reach for breath of air.

The void, an endless space,
Where echoes fade away.
In this forgotten place,
I yearn for light of day.

Yet courage finds a spark,
In whispers of the soul.
Against the endless dark,
I strive to feel more whole.

Through shadows, I will stand,
Embracing what is true.
In touching empty lands,
I find my path anew.

Ballet of the Breezes

Gentle whispers of the air,
Carrying secrets everywhere.
Leaves twirl, and branches sway,
Nature's dance in bright array.

A pirouette of sunlit rays,
Softly brushing through the haze.
Clouds drift by, a graceful waltz,
In the sky, where no one halts.

The fragrance of jasmine drifts,
In the breeze, the spirit lifts.
Harmony in every beat,
Nature's rhythm, pure and sweet.

As twilight falls, the stars appear,
The nightingale sings soft and clear.
In twilight's grasp, the world spins round,
In this ballet, peace is found.

The Lift of the Spirit

With each new dawn, hope takes flight,
Chasing shadows, embracing light.
Every breath a chance to soar,
Finding joy, forevermore.

Mountain peaks that touch the sky,
Guide the soul that dares to try.
Winds of change, a gentle push,
In life's race, we do not rush.

Hearts will rise like eagles bold,
Stories of courage yet untold.
In the warmth of love's embrace,
Every challenge we will face.

Breathe in deep, let worries fade,
In this life, love won't invade.
Together, hand in hand we fly,
Underneath the vast, blue sky.

Tales from High Above

The mountains whisper ancient lore,
Echoes from forevermore.
Clouds drift softly, mysteries weave,
In the sky, we dare believe.

Stars have seen the worlds unfold,
Every secret, every gold.
From heights where dreams and hopes reside,
Across the universe, we glide.

The winds carry our stories far,
Guiding us like a shooting star.
In each heartbeat, the past awakes,
A timeless journey, what it makes.

As night descends, the sky will glow,
Painted tales for us to know.
In the silence, wisdom calls,
From high above, as nightfall falls.

Dancing with the Zephyrs

Softly sings the morning breeze,
Rustling leaves on radiant trees.
A gentle touch, a sweet caress,
Whirling spirits, we are blessed.

In fields of gold, we sway and glide,
Nature's partner, side by side.
With every twirl, we feel the song,
The world spins fast, but we belong.

In twilight's glow, we find our place,
Where dreams take wing, a warm embrace.
As starlit skies begin to show,
We dance with zephyrs, fast and slow.

With moments fleeting, every kiss,
We trace the lines of boundless bliss.
Together twirling, spirits high,
In the arms of night's soft sigh.

Driftwood Dreams

On the shore where shadows play,
Driftwood whispers tales of old,
Waves embrace in soft ballet,
As sunsets bleed in shades of gold.

Caught between the sand and sea,
Dreams like ships adrift in time,
Tides will carry thoughts to me,
In rhythms of a subtle rhyme.

Nature's art, a fleeting glance,
Carved by storms and gentle hands,
Each piece holds a hidden chance,
To find a home on distant sands.

Ebb and flow, the heart takes flight,
In driftwood dreams, we find our way,
Guided by the soft moonlight,
Until the dawn breaks into day.

Elysian Skies

Underneath the azure dome,
Clouds like cotton, soft and bright,
Whispers of eternal home,
Kissed by gentle rays of light.

Birds in flight trace arcs of grace,
Dancing high on golden beams,
In this vast and open space,
We chase down our wildest dreams.

Veils of sunset paint the night,
Stars emerge like jewels on silk,
In the calm, the heart feels light,
Sipping twilight's velvet milk.

Elysian skies, a canvas vast,
Where worries fade and hopes arise,
In this moment, free at last,
We soar beneath the endless skies.

Chiaroscuro Emotions

In light and shadow, secrets hide,
A dance of joy, a veil of fear,
Moments sweet, while sorrows bide,
The heart's true depth feels ever near.

Laughter rings, a fleeting spark,
Yet tears may follow in their wake,
Colors clash within the dark,
A tapestry the soul must make.

Lost and found in black and white,
The shades where memories collide,
In every loss, there's hidden light,
A bittersweet and woven ride.

Chiaroscuro paints the path,
With brushstrokes of the heart's delight,
Through every joy and every wrath,
We find ourselves in the twilight.

The Weight of Altitude

Ascending peaks where eagles fly,
Breathless moments fill the air,
Clouds beneath, the world awry,
Freedom found in altitude's glare.

Echoes ring through canyons deep,
Whispers of the mountains' tales,
The weight of dreams, the heights we keep,
In silence where the spirit sails.

Each step a prayer, a vow to climb,
To touch the sky, to claim the dawn,
Against the odds, we beat in time,
Carving paths as we press on.

The weight of altitude we bear,
A burden blessed, a sacred quest,
In lofty realms, our hearts lay bare,
Finding solace in each conquest.

Fleeting Tranquility

In the hush of dawn's embrace,
Whispers of peace begin to trace.
Softly blooms the temporary,
Moments lost, yet not ordinary.

Gentle waves kiss the shore,
Echoes of a tranquil lore.
Leave behind the clamor loud,
In silence, solace is avowed.

With each breath, the stillness flows,
A fleeting dance, serenity knows.
Catch the light in fragile hands,
In this calm, the heart understands.

As daylight fades, shadows blend,
A tranquil heart learns to mend.
Embrace the night with quiet grace,
In fleeting moments, find your place.

Clouds of Introspection

Above the world, the thoughts take flight,
Drifting gently, soft and light.
In the mind, reflections sway,
Clouds obscure the bright of day.

Layers deep, the echoes ring,
Whispers of what silence brings.
Shapes of dreams on skies of gray,
In shadows, hidden truths lay.

As the storms begin to clear,
A brighter vision will appear.
Listen closely to the breeze,
In its dance, discover ease.

With every cloud that wanders near,
Thoughts congeal, yet disappear.
In introspection's gentle sway,
Life's true essence finds its way.

Navigating the Winds

With sails unfurled, the journey starts,
Guided by the beating hearts.
Each gust a tale, each shift a sign,
Carrying us through the divine.

The compass spins, yet we remain,
Aligned with hope amidst the strain.
On choppy seas, our spirits soar,
Together brave, we seek the shore.

Beneath vast skies, our dreams entwined,
In every wave, a truth defined.
Navigating through the storms we face,
Finding courage in our grace.

Though winds may howl and skies turn dark,
We'll chart our course, ignite the spark.
Through trials faced, we learn to trust,
In winds of change, we find our must.

Lightness of Being

In the meadow, a gentle sway,
Life whispers low, come out and play.
Every petal holds a gleam,
Embracing joy like a waking dream.

Floating free on currents bright,
In the dance of day and night.
Laughter echoes, spirits rise,
In this moment, boundless skies.

With hearts unburdened, we explore,
The lightness found at nature's core.
In every glance, a spark ignites,
Illuminating soul's delights.

With each embrace of life's sweet breeze,
We learn to wander, love, and seize.
In lightness woven, we transcend,
A tapestry that knows no end.

Fluttering Between Worlds

In twilight's grasp, we weave and dance,
Two realms unite, a fleeting chance.
With whispered dreams, we soar so high,
The pulse of life, a lullaby.

The stars align, the moon's embrace,
A secret place, where shadows chase.
In every breath, a story told,
Of fleeting love, both brave and bold.

Awake we are, in this bright haze,
The fireflies glow in gentle blaze.
We drift like leaves, on whispered streams,
Two worlds collide, within our dreams.

With every heartbeat, time suspends,
In twilight's glow, the magic bends.
We flutter soft, like silken threads,
Between the worlds where spirit treads.

Beneath the Feathered Veil

Soft whispers brush the morning sky,
Where dreams take flight and hopes can fly.
Feathers fall, like drops of rain,
Each one a tale of love and pain.

Beneath the veil, the secrets lie,
In silken folds of days gone by.
With every rustle, hearts ignite,
In shadows danced, we find our light.

The gentle touch of wings unfurled,
Embraced within this tender world.
A tapestry of hopes combined,
In each fine stitch, our fates entwined.

Beneath the feathered veil, we share,
The whispers soft, the silent prayer.
In this cocoon, we gently lay,
And let the dawn embrace the day.

Chasing the Invisible

Fingers grasp at shadows drawn,
A dance of light before the dawn.
With every step, the echoes tease,
The unseen dreams that glide like breeze.

In whispered thoughts, we chase the night,
The fragile glow of lost delight.
We run through fields of silver mist,
Where dreams and doubts do coexist.

The fleeting moments fade away,
Yet hope persists, a bright array.
In silent corners, secrets hide,
As we learn to embrace the tide.

Chasing the invisible, we find,
The threads of fate are intertwined.
In shadows cast, we'll leave our mark,
In every beat, a vibrant spark.

Celestial Expressions

Stars whisper secrets, soft and clear,
Painting the night with tales we hear.
Each twinkle holds a heart's desire,
In cosmic dreams, we never tire.

Galaxies swirl in vibrant hues,
Mapping the paths of ancient views.
With every glance, a spark ignites,
Illuminating the darkest nights.

Upon the canvas of the sky,
Celestial wonders brave and spry.
In silent awe, we watch and weave,
The tapestry of what we believe.

Expressions born in stardust bright,
Guiding souls through the endless night.
With every heartbeat, we embrace,
The universe's vast, warm grace.

Emotions on the Breeze

Gentle whispers brush the trees,
Carrying secrets on the breeze.
Soft laughter dances through the air,
Fleeting moments, light as fair.

Sunset colors paint the skies,
Fading daylight, soft goodbyes.
A sigh escapes, a heart takes flight,
Emotions soaring, pure delight.

Clouds like thoughts drift ever near,
Chasing shadows, losing fear.
Each heartbeat sways to nature's tune,
Under the watchful gaze of the moon.

In silence held, a story told,
Of love and dreams and hearts of gold.
Time flows gently, like a stream,
Carrying hope, embracing dreams.

Soaring Heartstrings

Tugging gently, heartstrings play,
Melodies of night and day.
In every rhythm, every sigh,
Lies the courage to fly high.

Whispers echo, dreams ignite,
Guiding paths in darkest night.
With every note, we break our chains,
Soaring free through joys and pains.

Through valleys deep and mountains tall,
Love's sweet harmony will call.
Together we can touch the stars,
Forging futures, healing scars.

In this dance, we find our truth,
A timeless bond, a song of youth.
Soaring heartstrings, tied so tight,
Forever reaching for the light.

Chasing Distant Dreams

In the twilight, shadows play,
Chasing dreams that slip away.
With open hearts and hopeful eyes,
We wander far beneath the skies.

Footsteps echo on this road,
Carrying burdens, lightening load.
Stars above, a guiding spark,
Leading us through the endless dark.

Each vision calls, a sweet embrace,
In whispered winds, we find our place.
Through valleys thick and mountains steep,
We hold the dreams we vow to keep.

Together, hand in hand we fly,
With every leap, we touch the sky.
Chasing distant dreams, we find,
The strength and joy in heart and mind.

Elevation of the Soul

Rising high on hopes anew,
Finding strength in all we do.
With every breath, we lift our gaze,
In unity, we share our days.

Mountains rise, and valleys yawn,
Through the darkness, we press on.
In every struggle, wisdom grows,
A journey where our spirit glows.

Through challenges, we learn to stand,
Together, forging a stronger band.
In every tear, a lesson learned,
In every flame, the heart has burned.

Elevation found in love,
Connecting with the stars above.
As we ascend, our spirits sing,
Embracing life, our souls take wing.

Spheres of Contentment

In the garden, dreams bloom bright,
Where whispers dance in soft daylight.
A tranquil heart, a gentle pace,
In warmth and love, we find our space.

With every breath, the worries cease,
A silent prayer for inner peace.
The world outside, a distant sound,
In stillness, joy is always found.

Beneath the stars, we share a sigh,
Time drifts like clouds across the sky.
Together here, we spread our wings,
In spheres of joy, contentment sings.

In laughter's echo, find your way,
Embrace the light of every day.
With open hearts, we walk this line,
In simple moments, love we find.

Flying with Shadows

Beneath the moon, we chase the night,
In whispered dreams, we take to flight.
With shadows close, we weave and sway,
Together, lost in twilight play.

Each step we take, the echoes call,
In secret paths, we rise and fall.
Through tangled woods, we find our way,
With shadows dancing, come what may.

The stars aligned, we glimpse the dawn,
With shadows' grace, our fears are gone.
In every heartbeat, freedom grows,
As twilight wraps us in its prose.

To dance with shadows, feel the breeze,
In flight with night, we find heart's ease.
Away we go, our spirits soar,
With love and light, forevermore.

Rapture in the Atmosphere

Up high we float, on clouds of dreams,
In golden hues, with sunlit beams.
A swirl of laughter, joy anew,
In rapture found, just me and you.

With every heartbeat, pulse entwined,
In boundless skies, our souls aligned.
Through layers thick, our spirits climb,
In rapture's glow, we pause for time.

The breezes hum a sweet refrain,
As gentle whispers kiss the rain.
With every breath, together, we,
In rapture's bond, we are set free.

In twilight's hush, the stars awake,
With every flicker, hearts then take.
A dance of light in atmosphere,
In rapture's realm, we find no fear.

Temptation of the Skies

The horizon calls, a sweet delight,
Where earth meets dreams in soft twilight.
With winds of change, we lift our sails,
In whispered hopes, adventure hails.

Beneath the stars, we chase the light,
In cosmic trails, our souls take flight.
With every glance, the sky implores,
In endless blue, temptation roars.

Through clouds that kiss the mountain tops,
In endless dance, our spirit hops.
With skies aglow in colors bright,
We chase the dawn, igniting night.

In moments shared, our laughter flies,
Together lost, beneath the skies.
With hearts afire, we long to roam,
In skies' embrace, we find our home.

Hearts in the Above

In twilight's glow, our dreams take flight,
Whispers of love in the soft moonlight.
Stars align, a dance divine,
Holding secrets, your heart in mine.

A gentle breeze through branches sighs,
Promising whispers, no goodbyes.
Hearts in the above, we shall reside,
In the warmth of night, with love our guide.

Floating clouds, our thoughts entwined,
Two wandering souls, forever aligned.
Through the canvas of the sky so bright,
Painting moments 'til the morning light.

In silence, our promises bloom and grow,
Tales of devotion in the starlit glow.
Together we weave our unbroken thread,
Hearts in the above, onward we tread.

Ethereal Echoes

In the mist of dreams, we softly tread,
Where echoes of whispers dance in our head.
Floating petals, alight in the stream,
Carrying love like a whispered dream.

Voices of shadows linger and play,
In the heart's caverns, where silence will sway.
Each heartbeat resonates, softly it flows,
Ethereal echoes, where true love grows.

Clouds undulate like a lover's sigh,
In the twilight of dusk, where wishes fly.
Glimmers of hope sparkle in the night,
Ethereal echoes, our souls take flight.

With every heartbeat, a tale unfolds,
In the garden of dreams, rich and bold.
Through time and space, forever we roam,
In ethereal echoes, we find our home.

Skimming the Surface of Desire

In a sea of dreams, we gently glide,
Skimming the surface, where yearnings bide.
Waves whisper secrets as they crash and swell,
Dancing on edges, casting our spell.

Underneath stars, our spirits soar,
Searching for treasures upon the shore.
Hand in hand, in the moonlit mist,
Seeking the magic that love can't resist.

Every heartbeat a ripple, a pulse anew,
Colors entwining, in shades of blue.
Skimming the surface, truth's glimmering fire,
Sailing forever on skiffs of desire.

With every glance, the world fades away,
In a symphony sweet, where hearts sway.
Together we dance, lost in the night,
Skimming the surface, our souls take flight.

Alchemy of Air and Heart

In the alchemy of air, our spirits blend,
Turning whispers to warmth, where dreams extend.
A dance of shadows, light and dark,
With every heartbeat, we ignite the spark.

Breezes carry secrets, unspoken and clear,
In the fragile stillness, I hold you near.
Together we forge our ethereal art,
In the alchemy of air, we embrace the heart.

Moments collide, like stars that ignite,
Creating constellations in the velvet night.
With your laughter, the world comes alive,
In this alchemy, our hearts will thrive.

Each breath a promise, a bond we shape,
In the tapestry woven, there's no escape.
Together forever, as lovers embark,
In the alchemy of air and the depths of heart.

The Call of the Gale

Whispers dance upon the breeze,
Calling forth the ancient trees.
Echoes of a stormy flight,
Guiding souls into the night.

Winds that carry tales untold,
Secrets from the brave and bold.
Lifted voices, wild and free,
Nature's song, a melody.

Racing clouds, a fleeting form,
Through the heat, formless and warm.
In the dark, a symphony,
The gale sings its remedy.

Beyond the hills, the shadows creep,
In the night, the earth will weep.
Yet through the heart, a fire glows,
The call of the gale ever flows.

Swaying in the Current

Down the stream, the waters sigh,
Beneath the vast and open sky.
Ripples play with gentle grace,
Time slows down in this embrace.

Branches dip and dance along,
Nature hums a soothing song.
Fish dart through the crystal cool,
Life unfolds, a vibrant jewel.

Sunlight kisses every wave,
Ancient rhythms, bold and brave.
In the flow, our cares release,
Swaying gently, finding peace.

Lost in dreams where currents lead,
In the depths, our spirits freed.
The river's path, a winding thread,
Sways our hearts as we are led.

Dance of the Larks

Up above, the larks they soar,
Singing sweetly, evermore.
In the dawn, their voices rise,
Painting joy across the skies.

Flashing feathers, bright and bold,
Stories of the days of old.
Curved in arcs, they spin and twirl,
Over fields, around the whirl.

Each note carries whispers far,
Underneath the morning star.
Hearts align with every song,
In their joy, we all belong.

As the sun begins to climb,
In their dance, we find our rhyme.
With the larks, we lift our hearts,
In this moment, life imparts.

Untamed Skies

Clouds that shift with wild intent,
Chasing dreams that never meant.
Vast horizons call us near,
In the silence, we shall steer.

Stars that blink, like distant flames,
Whisper softly, calling names.
Galaxies, a painted view,
In their depths, we find the true.

As the twilight paints its hue,
Awakens hope, our spirits new.
Breath of freedom, fierce and bright,
Guides us through the endless night.

Underneath the endless dome,
Wandering far, we find our home.
With each heartbeat, skies explore,
In the untamed, we'll soar once more.

A Sky of Whispered Secrets

Beneath the azure, wonders play,
Soft clouds dance in gentle sway.
A breeze carries tales untold,
In whispers new, in silence bold.

The sun dips low, a fiery hue,
Shadows stretch, embracing the view.
Stars awaken, shy at first,
In night's embrace, they quietly burst.

Moonlight glistens on the leaves,
Crickets sing as daylight weaves.
Rustling branches share their lore,
A sky of secrets, forevermore.

With every breath, the celestial speaks,
In twilight's grace, the heart seeks.
This canvas vast, we paint our dreams,
In whispered skies, where magic gleams.

Wings of Euphoria

Through open skies, our spirits glide,
On wings of light, we shall reside.
With every beat, a joyous song,
Together in the dance, where we belong.

Clouds embrace us, soft and white,
As colors blend in pure delight.
The sun ignites with golden rays,
In laughter's echo, our souls ablaze.

We soar above the world's demands,
With freedom's touch, we take our stands.
In every moment, love takes flight,
Wings of euphoria, hearts ignite.

And as the stars begin to gleam,
We find our way through every dream.
In this vast space, we'll always roam,
Together, friends, we build our home.

Celestial Yearnings

In night's embrace, our wishes rise,
A tapestry of endless skies.
Each twinkling star, a silent plea,
In cosmic realms, we long to be.

The moonlight bathes our hopes in gold,
Whispers of dreams, both brave and bold.
With stardust trails, we chart our way,
In celestial realms, forever stay.

Time drifts slowly, lost in time,
In every heartbeat, a silent rhyme.
Across the heavens, our spirits dance,
In cosmic currents, we take a chance.

So let us soar on wings of grace,
Embracing all this wondrous space.
In celestial yearnings, we are found,
Together in the starlit sound.

Above the Horizon's Veil

A canvas stretched from sea to shore,
The horizon whispers, forevermore.
Beneath the sun's embrace, we stand,
Eager to touch this foreign land.

In dawn's light, the world awakes,
With every pulse, the beauty shakes.
Colors burst and shadows flee,
A promise new, a mystery.

Above the veil, the heavens sigh,
Endless wonders flutter and fly.
We chase the dreams outside the frame,
In every heart, a burning flame.

As evening falls and stars adorn,
The night unfolds as hope is born.
Above the horizon, we will sail,
In whispered tales, our spirits trail.

Echoes of the Heart

In shadows deep where silence dwells,
Soft whispers linger, untold spells.
Each beat a song, a haunting trace,
A melody lost in time and space.

Through corridors of dreams we roam,
Connection felt, yet far from home.
Memories dance on the edge of night,
In every heartbeat, another light.

The pulse of longing, a gentle tide,
In every echo, love does abide.
Through valleys low and mountains tall,
We hear the heart's relentless call.

So let the echoes guide our way,
Through every night and into day.
In this sweet symphony of grace,
We'll find together our right place.

Chasing the Horizon

With every dawn, we rise anew,
Chasing dreams in shades of blue.
The world unfolds, a canvas wide,
With hopes and fears side by side.

Through hills and valleys, we push on,
With eyes set firm upon the dawn.
Each step a scribble, a story sung,
A dance of life, forever young.

The horizon beckons, a distant flame,
A whispered promise, a lover's name.
With every heartbeat, we draw near,
To chase the sun, to hold it dear.

So let us wander, hand in hand,
Through shifting tides of sea and sand.
For in the chase, our spirits soar,
Together bound, forevermore.

Enigmatic Skies

Beneath the vast, a mystery grows,
Through twilight hues, the soft wind blows.
Stars awaken, a cosmic sight,
In whispers of dusk, the dreams take flight.

Clouds drift softly, a painter's hand,
Crafting stories across the land.
Each star a wish, each moon a sigh,
In the enigma where secrets lie.

Through storms we wander, lost yet found,
In every pulse, the universe sounds.
Galaxies spin in timeless dance,
In the shadows, we find our chance.

Lift your gaze to the endless night,
Embrace the unknown, hold it tight.
For in the skies, our hopes reside,
In enigmatic realms, we abide.

Whispers of Freedom

Through open fields where wildflowers sway,
The whispers of freedom beckon to play.
With every breeze, a gentle call,
For hearts unchained, who dare to fall.

In the rustle of leaves, the secrets sing,
Of dreams unfurling on restless wing.
Each moment stretches, as time defies,
In the light of dawn, the spirit flies.

Bold are the souls who chase the sun,
For in their laughter, the battles won.
Through valleys deep and mountains high,
They find their voice, together they fly.

So let us dance, unbound, free,
In the rhythm of life, just you and me.
For in these whispers, we clearly see,
The essence of all that's meant to be.

Sails of Serenity

In the quiet of the sea,
The sails embrace the light,
Whispers of a gentle breeze,
Guiding dreams in flight.

Sunset paints the sky,
With colors soft and warm,
Nature's calm lullaby,
A peaceful, soothing charm.

Waves dance in harmony,
O'er the canvas vast and wide,
Every heartbeat's melody,
In the ocean's stride.

Drifting on the tides,
With hope and grace we soar,
In the sails of serenity,
We long for evermore.

The Pulse of the Breeze

Beneath the twilight glow,
The whispers softly call,
A rhythm in the air,
Nature's pulse enthralls.

Leaves sway in gentle curves,
As if to dance along,
They carry secret dreams,
In the evening's song.

With each caress of wind,
Our spirits start to rise,
A connection so profound,
Beneath the starlit skies.

Breath of life surrounds us,
In the ebb and flow we find,
The pulse of the breeze,
Forever intertwined.

Ascending Whimsy

Upwards towards the sky,
A kite begins to soar,
With colors bright and free,
It dances more and more.

Each string a whispered wish,
Floating high with delight,
Embracing every dream,
In the gentle light.

Clouds play the perfect game,
As shadows chase the sun,
An adventure waits ahead,
For souls that wish to run.

In the realm of whimsy,
Where laughter knows no bound,
We rise above the earth,
In pure joy, we're unbound.

Surrender to the Wind

Close your eyes and breathe,
Let go of all your fears,
For in the arms of wind,
Harmony appears.

It carries away troubles,
On its soft, caressing flight,
Bringing solace to the heart,
In the depth of night.

Feel the strength around you,
Trust the pathways na'ertaken,
In surrender there is power,
In freedom, dreams awaken.

So embrace the unseen,
Let it whisper through your soul,
In surrender to the wind,
You will find your whole.

Horizons of Unrest

Beneath the sky's vast, shifting hue,
Waves of doubt crash and break anew.
Voices echo in shadows cast,
A yearning for peace that can't seem to last.

Silent cries drift on restless winds,
Hope ignites where darkness begins.
In the distance, a flicker of light,
A promise of calm in the depth of the night.

Rivers of change flow through the land,
Unspoken dreams slip through our hands.
Yet in the chaos, we still seek grace,
Finding solace in our shared space.

The horizon calls, with whispers so sweet,
Inviting us closer to where hearts meet.
With each step forward, we face the test,
Embracing the journey, we lay down our unrest.

Stratospheric Sentiments

In the heights where the eagles soar,
Feelings dance, forever wanting more.
Clouds of longing drift and play,
Painting skies with dreams of the day.

Voices drift in the gentle breeze,
Fleeting moments that aim to please.
Stars above whisper soft refrains,
Declaring passions, freeing our chains.

Each heartbeat resonates like thunder,
In this vastness, we seek to wander.
With every breath, we chase the sublime,
In the fabric of love, we weave our rhyme.

Under celestial vaults we find our way,
In the tapestry of night and day.
Boundless feelings, eternally spun,
Stratospheric love, two become one.

Pathways of the Heart

Winding roads beneath the trees,
Whispers float on the fragrant breeze.
Every turn leads to what we crave,
Steps into pathways, brave and grave.

Gentle moments, hand in hand,
Together we learn to understand.
In each silence, a world unfolds,
Stories of love in amber and gold.

The heart's journey is often steep,
Yet in the valleys, we find what we keep.
Side by side, through shadows we stride,
On these pathways, our spirits abide.

With every choice, a step towards light,
Guided by stars that shine so bright.
In the quiet, we find our part,
Navigating the pathways of the heart.

The Apex of Emotion

At the summit where feelings collide,
Waves of passion we cannot hide.
Every heartbeat a thunderous call,
Echoing love, together we fall.

Cascading tears like summer rain,
Healing sorrows, embracing pain.
In the dance of joy and despair,
We find our strength, we learn to care.

Mountains rise, and rivers flow,
In the heart's echo, all lovers know.
Climbing higher with each embrace,
In the apex, we find our place.

Through the tempest, we chart a course,
Riding waves of unyielding force.
In this apex, emotions run free,
Here lies the truth of you and me.

Horizons Unbound

Beyond the hills, the sun will rise,
Colors merge in open skies.
Whispers of dreams, and tales untold,
With every dawn, new paths unfold.

Waves of golden light cascade,
In the heart, the fears will fade.
Chasing shadows, brave and bold,
In every step, we break the mold.

Fields of flowers, bright and wild,
Nature's canvas, serene and mild.
Breathe the freedom, taste the air,
With open hearts, beyond compare.

Horizons endless, futures bright,
Every heartbeat feels just right.
Together we will chase the morn,
In boundless dreams, a world reborn.

Serenade of the Soul

In quiet nights, the stars will sing,
Soft lullabies that dreams can bring.
Moonlight dances on the sea,
Cascading waves, wild and free.

Whispers linger in the breeze,
Echoing through ancient trees.
With every note, a heart will soar,
Seeking beauty, wanting more.

Among the shadows, melodies flow,
Telling stories only we know.
Filling spaces, dimmed by fear,
Creating magic, drawing near.

Let the music guide the way,
Carving paths of light and play.
In this serenade, we find our grace,
A timeless dance, our sacred space.

Ascent of Hope

Climbing mountains, step by step,
With every breath, our spirits leapt.
Holding tight to dreams so bright,
Through the darkness, seeking light.

Rivers rush with tales of old,
In their currents, hearts unfold.
Finding strength in every fall,
Rising up, we hear the call.

With every sunrise, shadows fade,
In the dawn, our fears are laid.
With open hearts, we find our way,
In the hope of a new day.

Ascent of hope, a brave endeavor,
Together we will conquer forever.
In unity, we share the climb,
Reaching heights, transcending time.

Turbulent Joy

In wild winds, our laughter flies,
Chasing storms, beneath the skies.
Colors clash in thunder's roar,
Yet in the chaos, we want more.

Heartbeats race with every gust,
In every moment, feel the thrust.
Whirling dances, pure delight,
In turbulent joy, we take flight.

Waves crashing on the rocks of fate,
In every challenge, we create.
Embrace the whirlwind, fear not the fall,
For in the tempest, we find our call.

Together we will ride the tide,
In glorious chaos, there's no need to hide.
Turbulent joy, a fierce embrace,
In every storm, we find our place.

Uplifted Spirits

In the morning light we rise,
Chasing shadows from our eyes.
With each step our hearts ignite,
Guided by the warmth of light.

Above the clouds, our dreams will soar,
With hope and joy, we'll seek for more.
Lifting spirits, we unite,
Fueling the fire, chasing the bright.

Every whisper of the breeze,
Bringing peace, we find our ease.
Together in this vibrant dance,
We embrace our life's sweet chance.

Through the trials, we will thrive,
Uplifted souls, we feel alive.
In gratitude, we raise a cheer,
For every moment, precious, dear.

Windborne Whispers

Gentle breezes through the trees,
Carry secrets, soft as pleas.
Nature speaks in rustling leaves,
Whispers wrapped in summer eves.

On mountain peaks where eagles fly,
Echoes linger in the sky.
Windborne tales of distant lands,
Kissed by time, in golden sands.

The ocean's breath, a soothing sound,
Waves of whispers all around.
From faraway, it calls us near,
In every hush, a song we hear.

Embrace the winds, let worries fade,
In their charms, our fears dismayed.
Windborne whispers guide our way,
A melody to light the day.

The Lift of Laughter

In a world where joy prevails,
Laughter dances, never fails.
With a giggle and a grin,
Every heart begins to spin.

Shared moments, sweet and bright,
Echo laughter through the night.
Every chuckle lifts the soul,
Mending cracks, making us whole.

Laughter rings like chimes of gold,
Stories told, forever bold.
In the warmth of a friendly jest,
We find our home, we find our rest.

So let us laugh, both loud and free,
In this joy, we find our glee.
For in the lift of laughter's song,
Together is where we belong.

Sun-kissed Reflections

Golden rays on water dance,
Painting moments, lost in trance.
Sun-kissed cheeks and hearts aglow,
Waves of warmth, a gentle flow.

As daytime fades, the colors blend,
In twilight's hush, we find our friends.
Reflections spark in fading light,
Whispers of a day's delight.

Nature's canvas, rich and grand,
Holds the stories we've all planned.
In the stillness, let us pause,
Cherishing life, its wondrous cause.

So let the sun guide our fate,
In every moment, we create.
Sun-kissed dreams, together weave,
In this reflection, we believe.

Heartstrings in Motion

In the dance of twinkling stars,
Our hearts beat a tender song,
Pulling close those near and far,
Binding souls with love so strong.

Each whisper carried on the breeze,
Melodies of hope and grace,
Through wooded paths and gentle seas,
Together we find our rightful place.

With every laugh, our spirits soar,
In the light of the moon's embrace,
Our dreams become forevermore,
As we chase the dawn's warm face.

Through the storms and sunny days,
We navigate this journey bold,
Hand in hand, in love's warm blaze,
A story of hearts softly told.

Glimmers of the Infinite

Stars blink secrets in the night,
Whispers of the cosmos' lore,
Each one a spark of pure delight,
Guiding us to seek and explore.

In the vastness, colors blend,
Galaxies dance in cosmic grace,
Each moment flows, no start, no end,
A timeless waltz in endless space.

Dreams like comets trail and blaze,
Through the black, they leave their mark,
Inviting us to uncharted ways,
Illuminating paths from dark.

With every heartbeat, we are drawn,
To the beauty of the unknown,
In this realm, we are reborn,
In the glimmers we have grown.

A Sky Full of Hues

The sun spills gold on waking morn,
As clouds dance bright in soft embrace,
A canvas rich, from silence born,
Colors flutter, dreams interlace.

Beneath the arcs of orange blaze,
We find our thoughts take flight anew,
In every shade, our hearts amaze,
Painting life as skies imbue.

The hues of twilight softly sigh,
As stars emerge in velvet tides,
Each moment whispers, lift your eyes,
In painted realms, our spirit rides.

In the spectrum, we explore,
The depth of feelings, vast and wide,
Each color tells of love and more,
In every brushstroke, joy and pride.

A Voyage of Thought

Set sail upon a sea of dreams,
With thoughts like waves that rise and fall,
Navigating through the streams,
Chasing whispers, answering the call.

In the currents, wisdom flows,
Charting courses, bold and clear,
Through the calm and through the throes,
We discover all we hold dear.

The horizon beckons with new sights,
As stars align to guide our way,
With each dawn, we find new flights,
In every journey, hearts will stay.

As we voyage deep within,
Through fears and hopes, we rise and dive,
In the silence, we begin,
To understand what keeps us alive.

Soaring through Silent Skies

Wings unfurl in a quiet breeze,
Clouds embrace, a moment's peace.
Above the world where dreams take flight,
Finding solace in the light.

Whispers of winds through azure lanes,
Carrying hopes like gentle rains.
Every heartbeat a song unsung,
In this vastness where I'm young.

Stars emerge with twilight's grace,
Mapping constellations in this space.
Floating higher, fears dissolve,
In this sky, we can evolve.

Soaring free, the spirit glows,
In silent echoes, life bestows.
Above the world, I dare to tread,
In the silence, dreams are spread.

Kaleidoscope of Emotions

Colors swirl in the mind's eye,
Feelings shift like clouds in the sky.
A mosaic crafted with each sigh,
Life's complexities, we can't deny.

Joy bursts forth in radiant streams,
While sorrow whispers in quiet dreams.
Every hue tells a tale profound,
In this dance of emotions, we're bound.

Passion ignites like fire's embrace,
Hope glimmers softly, finding its place.
Navigating through highs and lows,
In this kaleidoscope, the heart knows.

With every twist, life's beauty grows,
Shades of laughter and pain bestows.
In this vibrant tapestry we weave,
An ode to feelings, we believe.

Rise of the Heart's Compass

In the stillness, whispers call,
A direction sought through rise and fall.
The heart beats strong, a guiding light,
Navigating through the darkest night.

With every choice, a path unfolds,
In the silence, our truth beholds.
Dreams awaken, the journey starts,
Following the pulse of yearning hearts.

Through valleys deep and mountains steep,
Lies the promise of hopes to keep.
Each turn reveals what we must see,
The compass of love will set us free.

Rise up, dear soul, embrace the quest,
Wherever you wander, find your rest.
As long as you trust the heart's sweet song,
You'll find where you always belong.

Skylarking with Shadows

In the twilight, shadows dance,
Casting dreams in a fleeting glance.
Laughter echoes through the night,
As we chase the stars in flight.

Fleeting silhouettes, we race along,
Swaying gently with the night's song.
In the moonlight, secrets play,
Skylarking where shadows sway.

Lurking whispers in the dark,
Igniting wishes with a spark.
In this magic, we find our way,
With shadows as our guide, we stay.

So let us roam where shadows lead,
In this dance, we find our seed.
Together in the dusk's embrace,
Skylarking through time and space.

Milton Keynes UK
Ingram Content Group UK Ltd.
UKHW020150291024
450401UK00007B/102